A Christmas Novena with Benedict XVI

Selections from the Writings of Pope Benedict XVI by Lucio Coco
Prayers by Anna Maria Cànopi

Libreria Editrice Vaticana

United States Conference of Catholic Bishops
Washington, D.C.

English translation copyright © 2006 Libreria Editrice Vaticana. All rights reserved.

Some Scripture texts in this work are taken from the *New American Bible* with Revised New Testament and Revised Psalms © 1991, 1986, 1970 Confraternity of Christian Doctrine, Washington, D.C., and are used by permission of the copyright owner. All rights reserved. No part of the *New American Bible* may be reproduced in any form without permission in writing from the copyright owner.

Excerpts from the *Lectionary for Mass for Use in the Dioceses of the United States of America, second typical edition* © 2001, 1998, 1997, 1986, 1970 Confraternity of Christian Doctrine, Inc., Washington, DC. Used with permission. All rights reserved. No portion of this text may be reproduced by any means without permission in writing from the copyright owner.

First printing, January 2011

ISBN 978-1-60137-126-8

CONTENTS

Introduction... v

Meditations and Prayers

Day 1: The Coming of the Lord..................... 1
Day 2: A God with a Human Face.................. 8
Day 3: In Silence................................... 17
Day 4: Believing................................... 25
Day 5: The Living House of God 35
Day 6: The Joyful Journey 44
Day 7: A Great God................................ 52
Day 8: In a Relationship with Jesus 60
Day 9: The Fulfillment of the Word................ 68

Appendix 76

A Christmas Novena with Benedict XVI

The littleness of God made man in the Child
of Bethlehem reveals the greatness of human
beings and the beauty of our dignity as children
of God and brothers and sisters of Christ.

Benedict XVI

In the Child of Bethlehem, the smallness of God-made-man
shows us the greatness of man and the beauty of our dignity as
children of God and brothers and sisters of Jesus.

INTRODUCTION

The meditations contained in *A Christmas Novena with Benedict XVI* have been drawn from and built upon the words of Pope Benedict. This book is a collection of his thoughts and reflections on Christmas as found in his homilies, speeches, and audiences. They have been organized into the nine days of the novena based on their content. The themes of the coming of the Lord, anticipation, silence, faith, and joy are interwoven with meditations on the mystery of the Incarnation and reflections on Joseph, Zechariah, John the Baptist, and Mary, who is "the 'dwelling place' of the Lord, a true 'temple' in the world and a 'door' through which the Lord entered upon the earth" (Homily at First Vespers on the First Sunday of Advent, November 26, 2005).

Within this fabric of the story and character web proper to Christmas, we can make out some of the specific attributes of the Holy Father's interpretation that constitute and define some of the underlying themes of his early pontificate. In the paradox of the Incarnation, he sees a God who took on a human face: that of Jesus Christ. In this way, he showed everyone in tangible and practical terms that the search for God cannot lead to an unknown, imagined, or invented God, but must attain to a God who has shown himself and his face in Jesus (see Address at the Meeting with the Young People of the Diocese of Rome in Preparation for the 21st World Youth Day, April 6, 2006).

"We would like to see Jesus," said some of the Greeks who had come to Jerusalem for the feast of the Passover (see Jn 12:20-22). The wise men sought the same thing when they set out to adore him, only to find that the infant King was quite different from their expectations (see Address at the Youth Vigil, August 20, 2005) and the face they were seeking was different than what they had imagined: "In the Child of Bethlehem, God revealed himself in the humility of the 'human form,' in the 'form of a slave,' indeed, of one who died on a cross" (Homily on the Solemnity of the Epiphany, January 6, 2006). They had to experience this Christian paradox directly and perceive God's most eloquent manifestation precisely in this hiddenness. They had to change their thinking about God and therefore about themselves. The God of the manger teaches them, as he teaches us, that we must learn to serve rather than be served, to give of ourselves ("no lesser gift would be sufficient for this King" [Address, August 20, 2005]), and that power is exercised not by force but by truth, goodness, forgiveness, and mercy: "God did not send twelve legions of angels to assist Jesus in the Garden of Olives" (Address, August 20, 2005). Thus God teaches us that we must learn to lose ourselves and in so doing find ourselves.

These are the same responses that Jesus gave to the Greeks who wished to see him: "Amen, amen, I say to you, unless a grain of wheat falls to the ground and dies, it remains just a grain of wheat; but if it dies, it produces much fruit. Whoever loves his life loses it, and whoever hates his life in this world will preserve it for eternal life" (Jn 12:24-25). The Gospel does not tell us whether those pilgrims listened or turned away, saddened by not having been able "to see Jesus." Something different happens in the mystery of the Nativity: with our Lady's "yes," her decision to do the will of God and give herself unconditionally to the Lord, she shows us Jesus before even giving birth to him, revealing the face of a new humanity. St. Augustine said that "before conceiving the Lord in her body, she had already conceived him in her soul." God imprints his own image in her, the image of him who sacrifices his divine majesty to become little in order that we might find and love him. In this manner, Pope Benedict says, she becomes "the anticipated figure and everlasting portrait of the Son" (Homily on the 40th Anniversary of the Closing of the Second Vatican Council, December 8, 2005).

The novena is complete with prayers written by Mother Anna Maria Cànopi especially for this purpose, accompanying us on the nine-day journey toward the Savior's birth. In them, we can perceive the life of our Church in prayer, our Church thinking of all her children, and our Mother interceding with the Son for us. In them, we see Mary's burst of energy as she travels to share the joy of the divine conception with Elizabeth, and we hear our Mother praying for all mothers who are expecting a child today, defending the invaluable gift of life from conception to natural death. There is a thought for everyone in these prayers, and everyone can feel touched in some way by these petitions. Everyone can identify with the need—stronger now more than ever—for silence, listening, and meditation. In the light of the Gospel and the mystery of the Incarnation, together in Christ's presence, we can recognize and interpret the more or less apparent weaknesses, doubts, critical situations, and needs sown throughout our difficult times.

The time of Advent tells each of us that "the Lord always wants to come through us" (Homily, November 26, 2005). He is asking us, like he asked Mary, if we are ready to give him our bodies, our time, and our existence. The Lord "knocks at the door of our hearts . . . He also seeks a living dwelling place in our personal lives" (Homily, November 26, 2005). Therefore, bolstered by this characteristic hope surrounding the coming of the Lord, may the Father grant "us, who are parched land, the gift of becoming fertile ground for a joyful and grace-filled maternity" (Mother Cànopi). During this time of preparation for Christmas, let us also ask the Lord for that proliferative grace that allows us to welcome Christ into our souls and lives and beyond: "Not only must we carry him in our hearts, but we must bring him to the world, so that we too can bring forth Christ for our epoch" (General Audience, February 15, 2006).

LUCIO COCO

Note: All quoted material, unless otherwise indicated, is authored by Pope Benedict XVI. Sources are available at the official Vatican Web site, www.vatican.va.

Meditations and Prayers

DAY 1
THE COMING OF THE LORD

December 16th

Liturgy of the Word
Sir 48:1-4, 9-11; Ps 79; Mt 17:10-13

Greeting

Celebrant: In the name of the Father, and of the Son, and of the Holy Spirit.
Assembly: Amen.

Celebrant: The grace and peace of Christ, Son of God and Son of Mary, be with all of you.
Assembly: And with your spirit.

Canticle of the Prophecies

(Latin pp. 76-77; English pp. 78-79)

Benedict XVI tells us:

"And since the first coming of Christ is at the center of the history of humanity and at its end, his glorious return, so every personal existence is called to be measured against him—in a mysterious and multiform way—during the earthly pilgrimage, in order to be found 'in him' at the moment of his return" (Homily, November 26, 2005).

The question about Elijah

✠ A reading from the holy Gospel according to
   Matthew 17:9a, 10-13

As they were coming down from the mountain,
    the disciples asked Jesus,
    "Why do the scribes say that Elijah must come first?"
He said in reply, "Elijah will indeed come and
    restore all things;
    but I tell you that Elijah has already come,
    and they did not recognize him but did to him whatever
        they pleased.
So also will the Son of Man suffer at their hands."
Then the disciples understood
    that he was speaking to them of John the Baptist.

The Gospel of the Lord.

Let us meditate together with Benedict XVI:

"Why do the scribes say that Elijah must come first?"

"We should ask ourselves what does 'coming of the Lord' mean? In Greek it is 'parousia,' in Latin 'adventus,' 'advent,' 'coming.' What is this 'coming'? Does it involve us or not? . . . This coming was unique: 'the' coming of the Lord. Yet there is not only the final coming at the end of time: in a certain sense the Lord always wants to come through us. And he knocks at the door of our hearts: are you willing to give me your flesh, your time, your life? This is the voice of the Lord who also wants to enter our epoch, he wants to enter human life through us. He also seeks a living dwelling place in our personal lives. This is the coming of the Lord. Let us once again learn this in the season of Advent: the Lord can also come among us" (Homily, November 26, 2005).

Topics for reflection and prayer

Guided by the words of the Pope, let us prepare for the coming of the Lord.

The people whom God loves are *watchful*. They are ready to receive God's Word through the announcement of his angel, and their lives are not closed in on themselves. Their hearts are open. In a certain sense, deep down, they are people who are waiting for something: ultimately, they are waiting for God (see Homily at Midnight Mass on the Solemnity of the Nativity of the Lord, December 24, 2005).

God loves everyone because we are all his children. Yet some people have closed their hearts, and his love cannot find a way to enter. They think they do not need God; they do not want him. *Watchfulness* means readiness: readiness to listen, readiness to begin the journey, and anticipation of the light that shows the way. This is what God desires. He seeks people whose hearts are open with anticipation so that his light can enter, and with it, his peace (see Homily, December 24, 2005).

"Answering God requires the believer to make that inner journey which leads him or her to an encounter with the Lord. The encounter is only possible if the person can open his or her heart to God, who speaks in the depths of the conscience. This requires *interiority*, *silence*, and *watchfulness* (Address to Newly Appointed Bishops, September 19, 2005 [emphasis added]).

"Mary . . . entirely expected the Lord's coming. She could not, however, have imagined how this coming would be brought about. Perhaps she expected a coming in glory. The moment when the Archangel Gabriel entered her house and told her that the Lord, the Savior, wanted to take flesh in her, wanted to bring about his coming through her, must have been all the more surprising to her. We can imagine the Virgin's apprehension. Mary, with a tremendous act of faith and obedience, said 'yes': 'I am the servant of the Lord.' And so it was that she became the 'dwelling place' of the Lord, a true 'temple' in the world and a 'door' through which the Lord entered upon the earth" (Homily, November 26, 2005).

"God . . . does not impose himself, he never uses force to enter, but asks, as a child does, to be welcomed. In a certain sense, God too presents himself in need of attention: he waits for us to open our hearts to him, to take care of him" (Address during a Visit to St. Martha's Dispensary in Vatican City, December 30, 2005).

Magnificat antiphon

(classical Latin and English forms)

Ecce Rex veniet, Dominus terrae,
et ipse auferet iugum captivitatis nostrae.

Behold, the King will come, the Lord of earth:
and he will take away the yoke of our captivity.

Magnificat

(Latin p. 80; English p. 81)

Repeat antiphon

Prayers of Intercession

The Advent season has reached its climax, and the coming of the Savior is now at hand. May our prayers and anticipation continue to intensify so that Christ may find a welcoming home in our hearts, a place where he can be born and shine his light and peace over the whole world. For this we pray:

℟. Come, Lord Jesus, we await you with hope.

1. Come, Lord Jesus, to fill the holy Church with your blessings. May she always be a welcoming home ready to take in all people seeking light and salvation. May the poor, the suffering, and those whose hearts have gone astray find support and comfort in her. We pray to you:

℟. Come, Lord Jesus, we await you with hope.

2. Come, Lord Jesus, to reconcile all peoples to one another. Before you, the meek and unarmed Child, may the grim clamor of weapons give way to the song of peace. May there no longer be antagonism and violence, but rather joy in sharing and in unity. We pray to you:

℟. Come, Lord Jesus, we await you with hope.

3. Come, Lord Jesus, to make family ties strong and stable. For you who are life itself, may every child that is born be welcomed as a gift, and may every life nearing its close be respected with tenderness. May every action be carried out with greater humility and gentleness, together with you who are love itself, in a spirit of generous and joyful service. We pray to you:

℟. Come, Lord Jesus, we await you with hope.

4. Come, Lord Jesus, to bring consolation to the many poor and underprivileged of the world. They have nothing to give you; accept their human suffering as a precious treasure in building your kingdom of justice, love, and peace. We pray to you:

℟. Come, Lord Jesus, we await you with hope.

5. Come, Lord Jesus, into our vigilantly waiting hearts! May your presence conquer our idleness, burn away all our sins, and give our every desire for good the power to accomplish it. By this, may you always find in us that "yes" of complete willingness to cooperate with the work of salvation, the same "yes" that you found in your Mother, Mary. We pray to you:

℟. Come, Lord Jesus, we await you with hope.

Concluding Prayer

Lord Jesus, Son of the Eternal Father,
you never grow tired
of knocking at the door to our heart,
so often closed by obstinacy.
Help us to grow in faith, hope, and love,
so we can learn how to intimately await you,
recognize your presence in every person,
and welcome you with respect and passionate charity
especially in the poor and suffering.
May you be praised and blessed forever and ever.
Amen.

DAY 2
A GOD WITH A HUMAN FACE

December 17th

Liturgy of the Word
Zep 3:14-18a; Is 12:1-6; Phil 4:4-7; Lk 3:10-18

Greeting

Celebrant: In the name of the Father, and of the Son, and of the Holy Spirit.
Assembly: Amen.

Celebrant: The grace and peace of Christ, Son of God and Son of Mary, be with all of you.
Assembly: And with your spirit.

Canticle of the Prophecies

(Latin pp. 76-77; English pp. 78-79)

Benedict XVI tells us:

Being a disciple of John the Baptist means being men and women who are searching, who share Israel's hope, and who want to know the Word of the Lord—the reality of the Lord's presence—more intimately. It means that we too must be men and women of faith and hope (see Audience, June 14, 2006).

The preaching of John the Baptist

✠ A reading from the holy Gospel according to
   Luke 3:10-18

The crowds asked John the Baptist,
    "What should we do?"
He said to them in reply,
    "Whoever has two cloaks
    should share with the person who has none.
And whoever has food should do likewise."
Even tax collectors came to be baptized and they said to him,
    "Teacher, what should we do?"
He answered them,
    "Stop collecting more than what is prescribed."
Soldiers also asked him,
    "And what is it that we should do?"
He told them,
    "Do not practice extortion,
    do not falsely accuse anyone,
    and be satisfied with your wages."

Now the people were filled with expectation,
    and all were asking in their hearts
    whether John might be the Christ.
John answered them all, saying,

"I am baptizing you with water,
 but one mightier than I is coming.
I am not worthy to loosen the thongs of his sandals.
He will baptize you with the Holy Spirit and fire.
His winnowing fan is in his hand to clear his threshing floor
 and to gather the wheat into his barn,
 but the chaff he will burn with unquenchable fire."
Exhorting them in many other ways,
 he preached good news to the people.

The Gospel of the Lord.

Let us meditate together with Benedict XVI:

He preached good news to the people

"The New Testament is truly 'Gospel,' the 'Good News' that brings us joy. God is not remote from us, unknown, enigmatic or perhaps dangerous. God is close to us, so close that he makes himself a child and we can informally address this God. . . . 'The true God exists and this true God is good, he loves us, he knows us, he is with us, with us even to the point that he took on flesh!' . . . This is the great joy that Christianity proclaims. Knowing this God is truly 'Good News,' a word of redemption" (Homily at the Roman Parish of Santa Maria Consolatrice, December 18, 2005).

Topics for reflection and prayer

Guided by the words of the Pope, let us discover the human face of God.

"The Western world . . . is a world weary of its own culture. It is a world that has reached the time when *there is no longer any evidence of the need for God*, let alone Christ, and when it therefore seems that humans could build themselves on their own. In this atmosphere of a rationalism closing in on itself and that regards the model of the sciences as the only model of knowledge, everything else is subjective" (Address at the Meeting with the Diocesan Clergy of Aosta, July 25, 2005 [emphasis added]), "but man cannot understand himself fully if he ignores God" (Address to the Participants of a Seminar on European Higher Education, April 1, 2005).

"Is there still a need for God? Is it still reasonable to believe in God? Is Christ merely a figure in the history of religion or is he truly the Face of God that we all need? Can we live to the full without knowing Christ?" In an age marked by the eclipsing of transcendence, we must reaffirm the simplicity and richness of our faith: "we believe that God exists, that God counts; but which God? A God with a face, a human face, a God who reconciles, who overcomes hatred and gives us the power of peace that no one else can give us" (Address, July 25, 2005).

"We must go on . . . in the certainty that the world cannot live without God, the God of Revelation—and not just any

God: we see how dangerous a cruel God, an untrue God can be—the God who showed us his Face in Jesus Christ. This Face of the One who suffered for us, this loving Face of the One who transforms the world" (Address, July 25, 2005). "The Incarnation, the Son of God becoming human, his entry into history, is the crowning point of God's revelation of himself to Israel and to all the peoples. In the Child of Bethlehem, God revealed himself in the humility of the 'human form'" (Homily on the Solemnity of the Epiphany, January 6, 2006).

"In vast areas of the world today there is a strange *forgetfulness of God*. It seems as if everything would be just the same even without him. But at the same time there is a feeling of frustration, a sense of dissatisfaction with everyone and everything" (Homily on the Occasion of the 20th World Youth Day, August 21, 2005 [emphasis added]). During this Advent season, let us proclaim the Good News of Jesus Christ like John the Baptist! "Let us seek to know him better and better, so as to be able to guide others to him with conviction" (Homily, August 21, 2005).

People do not know God; they do not know Christ. There is a new paganism, and it is not sufficient that we seek to preserve the existing flock—though this is important—because an important question stands out: what really is life? I believe we all need to find new ways of bringing the Gospel to the modern world, proclaiming Christ anew, and establishing the faith (see Homily, August 21, 2005). "It is therefore urgently necessary . . . to listen anew to the Gospel, the Word of the Lord, the word of truth, so that in every Christian, in every one of us, the understanding of the truth given to him, given to us, may be strengthened, so that we may live it and witness to it" (Audience, March 1, 2006).

Magnificat antiphon

(classical Latin and English forms)

O Sapientia, quae ex ore Altissimi prodisti,
attingens a fine usque ad finem,
fortiter suaviterque disponens omnia:
veni ad docendum nos viam prudentiae.

O Wisdom of our God Most High,
guiding creation with power and love:
come to teach us the path of knowledge.

Magnificat

(Latin p. 80; English p. 81)

Repeat antiphon

Prayers of Intercession

We are saddened every day by the news of devastating massacres, wars, and murderous hatred in every corner of the world. Yet today we are surprised by the Church's unwaveringly joyful proclamation: "rejoice, be glad, fear not, for the Lord is near, the Lord is coming!" With hearts full of hope, let us raise our confident prayers to Christ, the Icon of the Father:

℟. Come, Lord Jesus, show us the face of love.

1. We somberly recognize, Lord, that in our society with such advanced means of communication, dialogue has never been so difficult and feelings of loneliness and anguish have never been so rampant. May you who know our thirst for happiness grant us sight by faith, so that we might see the divine image in all human persons and establish true relationships as brothers and sisters. We pray to you with confidence:

℟. Come, Lord Jesus, show us the face of love.

2. Lord, bring forth many saintly vocations from within your Church. Help all Christians to ardently desire a more generous missionary drive, and to be intrepid witnesses always and everywhere to the joy of living the Gospel. We pray to you with confidence:

℟. Come, Lord Jesus, show us the face of love.

3. Lord, turn your merciful eyes to all persons of every tribe, tongue, people, and nation. You have come to be God-with-us, the Prince of Peace, and the Good Shepherd; gather us in unity and guide us toward knowing one another in the light of truth

and love, so that we might walk together toward the house of the Father. We pray to you with confidence:

℟. Come, Lord Jesus, show us the face of love.

4. We ask you, Lord, to fill all artists and academics with your Holy Spirit so that they may become passionate seekers and humble servants of the truth. Enamored with the mystery of life, may they learn the joy of letting the rays of your beauty and goodness shine on all people. We pray to you with confidence:

℟. Come, Lord Jesus, show us the face of love.

5. Having taken on yourself the burden of all human suffering, we ask you, Lord, to keep us strong in our faith and grant us the gifts of silent adoration and humble and sincere charity, so that every person in suffering may perceive your presence in us and be comforted by your gentle, loving gaze. We pray to you with confidence:

℟. Come, Lord Jesus, show us the face of love.

Concluding Prayer

O Father of infinite goodness,
you decide all things with loving wisdom.
After so much sinning, suffering, and seeking,

help all men and women of our time to discover
in the coming Christ
their identity as children of God,
the joy of spiritual childhood,
the freshness of genuine faith,
and the fidelity of mature and generous love,
so that we can build a society
truly imbued with Christian values.
Through Christ our Lord.
Amen.

DAY 3
IN SILENCE

December 18th

Liturgy of the Word
Jer 23:5-8; Ps 71; Mt 1:18-25

Greeting

Celebrant: In the name of the Father, and of the Son, and of the Holy Spirit.
Assembly: Amen.

Celebrant: The grace and peace of Christ, Son of God and Son of Mary, be with all of you.
Assembly: And with your spirit.

Canticle of the Prophecies

(Latin pp. 76-77; English pp. 78-79)

Benedict XVI tells us:

"[Joseph's] greatness, like Mary's, stands out even more because his mission was carried out in the humility and hiddenness of the house of Nazareth. Moreover, God himself, in the person of his Incarnate Son, chose this way and style of life—humility and hiddenness—in his earthly existence" (*Angelus*, March 19, 2006).

Joseph's dream

✠ A reading from the holy Gospel according to
   Matthew 1:18-25

This is how the birth of Jesus Christ came about.
When his mother Mary was betrothed to Joseph,
> but before they lived together,
> she was found with child through the Holy Spirit.

Joseph her husband, since he was a righteous man,
> yet unwilling to expose her to shame,
> decided to divorce her quietly.

Such was his intention when, behold,
> the angel of the Lord appeared to him in a dream and said,
> "Joseph, son of David,
> do not be afraid to take Mary your wife into your home.

For it is through the Holy Spirit
> that this child has been conceived in her.

She will bear a son and you are to name him Jesus,
> because he will save his people from their sins."

All this took place to fulfill
> what the Lord had said through the prophet:

> *Behold, the virgin shall be with child and bear a son,*
> *and they shall name him Emmanuel,*

which means "God is with us."
When Joseph awoke,
> he did as the angel of the Lord had commanded him
> and took his wife into his home.

He had no relations with her until she bore a son,
> and he named him Jesus.

The Gospel of the Lord.

Let us meditate together with Benedict XVI:

Joseph, Son of David, do not be afraid

"St. Joseph's silence does not express an inner emptiness but, on the contrary, the fullness of the faith he bears in his heart and which guides his every thought and action. It is a silence thanks to which Joseph, in unison with Mary, watches over the Word of God, known through the Sacred Scriptures, continuously comparing it with the events of the life of Jesus; a silence woven of constant prayer, a prayer of blessing of the Lord, of the adoration of his holy will and of unreserved entrustment to his providence. It is no exaggeration to think that it was precisely from his 'father' Joseph that Jesus learned—at the human level—that steadfast interiority which is a presupposition of authentic justice, the 'superior justice' which he was one day to teach his disciples (cf. Mt 5: 20). Let us allow ourselves to be 'filled' with St. Joseph's silence! In a world that is often too noisy, that encourages neither recollection nor listening to God's voice, we are in such deep need of it.

During this season of preparation for Christmas, let us cultivate inner recollection in order to welcome and cherish Jesus in our own lives" (*Angelus*, December 18, 2005).

Topics for reflection and prayer:

Guided by the words of the Pope, let us improve our capacity for silence, listening, and prayer.

"St. Joseph's *silence* does not express an inner emptiness but, on the contrary, the fullness of the faith he bears in his heart and which guides his every thought and action" (*Angelus*, December 18, 2005 [emphasis added]). He makes us aware that "without sufficient recollection it is impossible to approach the supreme mystery of God and of his revelation" (Audience, July 5, 2006).

"St. Joseph's *silence* . . . [is] a silence woven of constant prayer, a prayer of blessing of the Lord, of the adoration of his holy will and of unreserved entrustment to his providence" (*Angelus*, December 18, 2005 [emphasis added]). "Let us not be consumed with haste, as if time dedicated to Christ in silent prayer were time wasted. On the contrary, it is precisely then that the most wonderful fruits . . . come to birth" (Address at the Meeting with the Clergy in the Cathedral of St. John in Warsaw, May 25, 2006), "[in the] moving experience of prayer as dialogue with God, the God who we know loves us and whom we in turn wish to love" (Address at the Papal Welcoming Ceremony in Cologne, August 18, 2005).

Thanks to silence, "Joseph, in unison with Mary, *watches over the Word of God*, known through the Sacred Scriptures, continuously comparing it with the events of the life of Jesus"

(*Angelus*, December 18, 2005 [emphasis added]). "We should [learn to] know Jesus in an increasingly personal way, listening to him, living together with him, staying with him . . . that is, reading Sacred Scripture in a non-academic but spiritual way; thus, we learn to encounter Jesus present, who speaks to us. We must reason and reflect, before him and with him, on his words and actions. The reading of Sacred Scripture is prayer, it must be prayer—it must emerge from prayer and lead to prayer" (Homily at the Chrism Mass in St. Peter's Basilica, April 13, 2006).

"Mary [too] *treasures in her heart* the words that come from God and, piecing them together as in a mosaic, learns to understand them. Let us too, at her school, learn to become attentive and docile disciples of the Lord. With her motherly help, let us commit ourselves to working enthusiastically in the 'workshop' of peace, following Christ, the Prince of Peace" (Homily on the Solemnity of Mary, Mother of God, January 1, 2006 [emphasis added]).

Magnificat antiphon:

(classical Latin and English forms)

O Adonai, et Dux domus Israel,
qui Moysi in igne flammae rubi apparuisti
et ei in Sina legem dedisti:
veni ad redimendum nos in brachio extento.

O Leader of the House of Israel,
giver of the Law to Moses on Sinai:
come to rescue us with your mighty power!

Magnificat

(Latin p. 80; English p. 81)

Repeat antiphon

Prayers of Intercession

Along the road to the grotto in Bethlehem, today we encounter St. Joseph, a humble, silent, and faithful servant of the Lord, a just and God-fearing man who was chosen to be the adoptive father and guardian of the child Jesus. Continuing the Advent journey with him, let us bear his example in mind so that we will be ready to welcome the coming Lord. For this we pray:

℟. Grant us, Lord Jesus, the adoring silence of love.

1. O God, our gracious Father, we pray for our bishops, priests, and all religious called by you to cooperate more closely with the work of redemption. May they be people of great inner depth who draw the light and strength to serve you with absolute fidelity and self-denial from the Eucharist, thoughtful attention to your Word, fervent prayer, and contemplative silence. For this we pray:

℟. Grant us, Lord Jesus, the adoring silence of love.

2. We pray for those who have social and political responsibilities. Grant them your Spirit, so that they may never cease

the humble search for paths of reconciliation and peace among nations. May they always promote whatever fosters the true advancement of society and the human and spiritual growth of all persons. For this we pray:

℟. Grant us, Lord Jesus, the adoring silence of love.

3. We pray for all the poor and underprivileged of the world, for abandoned children and countless refugees, and for the elderly and the sick. O merciful Father who loves all his children, with the support of charity and prayers from the entire Church, may they every day find the strength to silently accept their trials through faith, confidently committing themselves to your hands. For this we pray:

℟. Grant us, Lord Jesus, the adoring silence of love.

4. We pray for all young men and women. Stir in their hearts a yearning for innocence, a love of silence and pure beauty, and a passion for holiness. In listening to and meditating upon your Word, help them to feel drawn toward higher ideals and to discover that the secret to true happiness is only in friendship with you and in turning life into a gift of service to others. For this we pray:

℟. Grant us, Lord Jesus, the adoring silence of love.

5. We pray for all of us gathered here. Help us to follow the example of Joseph and Mary, that we may learn how to keep

intact the treasure of faith with which you have entrusted us. May we be a charitable, meek, and peaceful presence to our brothers and sisters in the constant quest for good and communion with all. For this we pray:

℟. Grant us, Lord Jesus, the adoring silence of love.

Concluding Prayer

O God, Creator and Father,
you are the only Lord of the universe and of history.
With your Incarnate Word you desired to become
the "Emmanuel," the "God-with-us."
Help every man and woman, through deep inner silence,
to be listening for the signs of your will
and to experience, as part of your Church,
the comfort and strength
that come from confronting life's challenges
together, with mutual support.
Through Christ our Lord.
Amen.

DAY 4
BELIEVING

December 19th

Liturgy of the Word
Jgs 13:2-7, 24-25a; Ps 70; Lk 1:5-25

Greeting

Celebrant: In the name of the Father, and of the Son, and of the Holy Spirit.
Assembly: Amen.

Celebrant: The grace and peace of Christ, Son of God and Son of Mary, be with all of you.
Assembly: And with your spirit.

Canticle of the Prophecies

(Latin pp. 76-77; English pp. 78-79)

Benedict XVI tells us:

"God is hidden in mystery; to claim to understand him would mean to want to confine him within our thinking and knowing and consequently to lose him irremediably. With faith, however, we can open up a way through concepts, even theological concepts, and can 'touch' the living God. And God, once touched, immediately gives us his power" (Address at the Meeting with Men and Women Religious, Seminarians, Representatives of Movements and Consecrated Life at the Shrine of Jasna Góra, May 26, 2006).

The announcement of the birth of John the Baptist

✠ A reading from the holy Gospel according to Luke 1:5-25

In the days of Herod, King of Judea,
    there was a priest named Zechariah
    of the priestly division of Abijah;
    his wife was from the daughters of Aaron,
    and her name was Elizabeth.
Both were righteous in the eyes of God,
    observing all the commandments
    and ordinances of the Lord blamelessly.
But they had no child, because Elizabeth was barren
    and both were advanced in years.

Once when he was serving as priest
    in his division's turn before God,
    according to the practice of the priestly service,
    he was chosen by lot
    to enter the sanctuary of the Lord to burn incense.
Then, when the whole assembly of the people
    was praying outside
    at the hour of the incense offering,
    the angel of the Lord appeared to him,

standing at the right of the altar of incense.
Zechariah was troubled by what he saw, and fear came
> upon him.

But the angel said to him, "Do not be afraid, Zechariah,
> because your prayer has been heard.
Your wife Elizabeth will bear you a son,
> and you shall name him John.
And you will have joy and gladness,
> and many will rejoice at his birth,
> for he will be great in the sight of the Lord.
He will drink neither wine nor strong drink.
He will be filled with the Holy Spirit even from
> his mother's womb,
> and he will turn many of the children of Israel
> to the Lord their God.
He will go before him in the spirit and power of Elijah
> to turn the hearts of fathers toward children
> and the disobedient to the understanding of the righteous,
> to prepare a people fit for the Lord."

Then Zechariah said to the angel,
> "How shall I know this?
For I am an old man, and my wife is advanced in years."
And the angel said to him in reply,
> "I am Gabriel, who stand before God.
I was sent to speak to you and to announce to you this good news.
But now you will be speechless and unable to talk

> until the day these things take place,
> because you did not believe my words,
> which will be fulfilled at their proper time."

Meanwhile the people were waiting for Zechariah
> and were amazed that he stayed so long in the sanctuary.

But when he came out, he was unable to speak to them,
> and they realized that he had seen a vision in the sanctuary.

He was gesturing to them but remained mute.

Then, when his days of ministry were completed, he went home.

After this time his wife Elizabeth conceived,
> and she went into seclusion for five months, saying,
> "So has the Lord done for me at a time when he has seen fit
> to take away my disgrace before others."

The Gospel of the Lord.

Let us meditate together with Benedict XVI:

But now you will be speechless . . . because you did not believe my words.

"To believe means first to accept as true what our mind cannot fully comprehend. We have to accept what God reveals to us about himself, about ourselves, about everything around us, including the things that are invisible, inexpressible and beyond our imagination. This act of accepting revealed truth broadens the horizon of our knowledge and draws us to the mystery in which our lives are immersed. Letting our reason be limited in this way is not something easy to do. Here we see the second aspect of faith: it is trust in a person, no ordinary person, but Jesus Christ himself. What we believe is important, but even more important is the One in whom we believe" (Homily at the Mass in Błonie Park in Krakow, May 28, 2006).

Topics for reflection and prayer:

Guided by the words of the Pope, let us meditate on the meaning of faith.

Zechariah's incredulity teaches us the need to accept as true what our minds do not completely grasp; it teaches us to have faith. "Through faith we accept the gift that God makes of himself in revealing himself to us, creatures made in his image. We welcome and accept that Truth which our minds cannot fully comprehend or possess but which, for this very reason, extends the horizon of our knowledge and enables us to arrive at the Mystery in which we are immersed, and to find in God the definitive meaning of our lives" (Address to the Participants in the Ecclesial Convention of the Diocese of Rome, June 5, 2006; see Homily, May 28, 2006).

As openness to transcendence and to God, "faith is not merely the attachment to a complex of dogmas, complete in itself, that is supposed to satisfy the thirst for God, present in the human heart. On the contrary, it guides human beings on their way through time toward a God who is ever new in his infinity. Christians, therefore, are at the same time both seekers and finders. It is precisely this that makes the Church young, open to the future, rich in hope for the whole of humanity" (*Angelus*, August 28, 2005).

"Human existence is a journey of faith and as such, moves ahead more in shadows than in full light, and is no stranger to moments of obscurity and also of complete darkness. While we are on this earth, our relationship with God takes place more by listening than by seeing; and the same contemplation comes about, so to speak, with closed eyes, thanks to the interior light that is kindled in us by the Word of God" (*Angelus*, March 12, 2006).

"Zechariah . . . lost the ability to speak because he did not believe the angel, but subsequently, in pardoning him, God granted him the gift of prophecy in the hymn of the *Benedictus*: 'The one who could not speak now prophesies,' St. Ambrose said, adding that 'it is one of the greatest graces of the Lord, that those who have denied him should confess belief in him' (2, 33: *SAEMO, XI*, Milan-Rome, 1978, p. 175)" (Audience, October 19, 2005). "Faith can always bring us back to God even when our sin leads us astray" (Address, May 26, 2006). "A living faith must always grow" (Address at the Meeting with the Young People in Błonie Park, May 27, 2006). "To all for whom it is difficult to believe in God, I say again today: 'God is love.' Dear friends, be witnesses to this truth" (Address, May 26, 2006).

"Faith . . . [is] a fundamental attitude of the spirit, not merely something intellectual or sentimental; true faith involves the entire person: thoughts, affections, intentions, relations, bodiliness, activity and daily work" (Audience, May 31, 2006). "Discovering the beauty and joy of faith is a path that every new generation must take on its own, for all that we have that is most our own and most intimate is staked on faith: our heart, our mind, our freedom, in a deeply personal relationship with the Lord at work within us" (Address, June 5, 2006).

Magnificat antiphon:

(classical Latin and English forms)

O Radix Iesse,
qui stas in signum populorum,
super quem continebunt reges os suum,
quem gentes deprecabuntur:
veni ad liberandum nos, iam noli tardare.

O Root of Jesse's stem,
sign of God's love for all his people:
come to save us without delay!

Magnificat

(Latin p. 80; English p. 81)

Repeat antiphon

Prayers of Intercession

By presenting us with the person of Zechariah, today's liturgy invites us to welcome the renewing grace of this Advent season, which is the most perfect time to be amazed at God's ever new and wonderful surprises. May all humankind experience a new springtime of the spirit and rediscover the drive to build a society open to truly life-giving values. For this, we pray together with faith:

℟. Lord Jesus, come renew our faith.

1. With great joy and holy reverence, we carry in our hands the flame of faith that has shed light on the paths of history from generation to generation. Lord, we pray for the Church, your Bride: may she always radiate holiness and beauty so that all people will experience the attractiveness of the Gospel. For this we pray:

℟. Lord Jesus, come renew our faith.

2. Lord, we pray for those who have drawn away from the faith under trials of suffering, turning into themselves in an attempt to reject life. Make us able to be messengers to them, communicating your love that has given salvific power to suffering. Transforming their silent anguish into a prayerful cry, we ask you:

℟. Lord Jesus, come renew our faith.

3. Lord Jesus, we pray for our parents, teachers, catechists, and all those who are responsible for education. Help them to draw light and strength from prayer and an active sacramental life, that they may kindle a desire for profound communion with you in the hearts of young men and women. For this we pray:

℟. Lord Jesus, come renew our faith.

4. In solidarity with our brothers and sisters who are persecuted for their faith, we ask you, Lord, to make them true witnesses to your love. May they fight evil solely with the power of goodness and forgiveness, experience true peace in their hearts, and let the light of your presence shine through and around them. For this we pray:

℟. Lord Jesus, come renew our faith.

5. Lord, do not let the flame of our faith be extinguished by the tempestuous winds of disbelief and corruption. Grant that we may resist their raging gusts and await your Nativity with the silent provisions of prayer, simple charity, and unfailing hope. For this we pray:

℟. Lord Jesus, come renew our faith.

Concluding Prayer
Lord, our faithful God,
you always answer our prayers
by going beyond what we merit and desire.
Grant that we may await the hour of grace
with perseverance
even when you test us with your silence.
May the faithful Virgin Mary
help us to live this Advent
as a journey of inner purification,

that we may be strengthened in faith
and arrive this Christmas
ready to welcome the gift of salvation
with joy and thanksgiving.
Through Jesus Christ, our Lord.
Amen.

DAY 5
THE LIVING HOUSE OF GOD

December 20th

Liturgy of the Word
Is 7:10-14; Ps 23; Lk 1:26-38

Greeting

Celebrant: In the name of the Father, and of the Son, and of the Holy Spirit.
Assembly: Amen.

Celebrant: The grace and peace of Christ, Son of God and Son of Mary, be with all of you.
Assembly: And with your spirit.

Canticle of the Prophecies

(Latin pp. 76-77; English pp. 78-79)

Benedict XVI tells us:

Mary teaches us that "to love according to God it is necessary to live in him and of him: God is the first 'home' of human beings, and only by dwelling in God do men and women burn with a flame of divine love that can set the world 'on fire'" (Message for 80th World Mission Sunday 2006, April 29, 2006).

The announcement to Mary

✠ A reading from the holy Gospel according to
   Luke 1:26-38

In the sixth month,
> the angel Gabriel was sent from God
> to a town of Galilee called Nazareth,
> to a virgin betrothed to a man named Joseph,
> of the house of David,
> and the virgin's name was Mary.

And coming to her, he said,
> "Hail, full of grace! The Lord is with you."

But she was greatly troubled at what was said
> and pondered what sort of greeting this might be.

Then the angel said to her,
> "Do not be afraid, Mary,
> for you have found favor with God.

Behold, you will conceive in your womb and bear a son,
> and you shall name him Jesus.

He will be great and will be called Son of the Most High,
and the Lord God will give him the throne of
> David his father,
> and he will rule over the house of Jacob forever,
> and of his Kingdom there will be no end."

But Mary said to the angel,
> "How can this be,

    since I have no relations with a man?"
And the angel said to her in reply,
    "The Holy Spirit will come upon you,
    and the power of the Most High will overshadow you.
Therefore the child to be born
    will be called holy, the Son of God.
And behold, Elizabeth, your relative,
    has also conceived a son in her old age,
    and this is the sixth month for her who was called barren;
    for nothing will be impossible for God."

Mary said, "Behold, I am the handmaid of the Lord.
May it be done to me according to your word."
Then the angel departed from her.

The Gospel of the Lord.

Let us meditate together with Benedict XVI:

Hail, full of grace!

    "The first word on which I would like to meditate with you is the Angel's greeting to Mary. In the Italian translation the Angel says: 'Hail, Mary.' But the Greek word below, 'Kaire,' means in itself 'be glad' or 'rejoice' . . . This is the first word that resounds in the New Testament as such, because the Angel's announcement to Zechariah of the birth of John the Baptist is the word that still rings out on the threshold between the two Testaments. It is only with this dialogue which the Angel Gabriel has with Mary that the New Testament really begins. We can therefore say that the first word of the New Testament is an invitation to joy: 'rejoice, be glad!'" (Homily, December 18, 2005).

Topics for reflection and prayer:

Guided by the words of the Pope, let us make ready to say "yes" to the Lord like Mary.

"Mary, the humble provincial woman . . . is 'the holy remnant' of Israel to which the prophets referred in all the periods of trial and darkness. . . . In her the Lord *dwells*, in her he finds the place of his repose. She is the living house of God, who does not dwell in buildings of stone but in the heart of living man" (Homily, December 8, 2005 [emphasis added]). "Do not be content with external piety. God is not satisfied by the fact that his people pay him lip service. God wants their *hearts* and gives us his grace if we do not drift away or cut ourselves off from him" (Address to the Bishops of Austria on their "Ad Limina" Visit, November 5, 2005 [emphasis added]).

"Today . . . we contemplate this aspect of the Mystery—the divine wellspring flows through a privileged channel: the Virgin Mary. St. Bernard speaks of this using the eloquent image of *aquaeductus* (cf. *Sermo in Nativitate B.V. Mariae: PL* 183, 437-448). In celebrating the Incarnation of the Son, therefore, we cannot fail to honor his Mother. The Angel's proclamation was addressed to her; she accepted it, and when she responded from the depths of her heart: 'Here I am . . . let it be done to me according to your word' (Lk 1: 38), at that moment the eternal Word began to exist as a human being in time" (Homily at the Eucharistic Concelebration with the New Cardinals, March 25, 2006).

"Mary . . . accepts with *personal generosity* the wave of God's love poured out upon her. In this too, she is the perfect disciple of her Son, who realizes the fullness of his freedom and thus exercises the freedom through obedience to the Father" (Homily, March 25, 2006 [emphasis added]). "The person who abandons himself totally in God's hands does not become God's puppet, a boring 'yes man'; he does not lose his freedom. Only the person who entrusts himself totally to God finds true *freedom*, the great, creative immensity of the freedom of good" (Homily, December 8, 2005 [emphasis added]).

"The person who turns to God does not become smaller but greater, for through God and with God he becomes great, he becomes divine, he becomes truly himself. The person who puts himself in God's hands does not distance himself from others, withdrawing into his private salvation; on the contrary, it is only then that his heart truly awakens and he becomes a sensitive, hence, benevolent and open person. *The closer a person is to God, the closer he is to people*. We see this in Mary. The fact that she is totally with God is the reason why she is so close to human beings" (Homily, December 8, 2005 [emphasis added]).

"Mary is so interwoven in the great mystery of the *Church* that she and the Church are inseparable, just as she and Christ are inseparable. Mary mirrors the Church, anticipates the Church in her person, and in all the turbulence that affects the suffering, struggling Church she always remains the Star of salvation" (Homily, December 8, 2005 [emphasis added]). In an age when people seem to have no need of the Church and everything seems pointless, help us to learn from Mary that only the seed of the Word of the Lord always transforms the earth anew and opens it to true life (see Address, July 25, 2005).

Magnificat antiphon:

(classical Latin and English forms)

O Clavis David,
et sceptrum domus Israel,
qui aperis, et nemo claudit,
claudis, et nemo aperit:
veni, et educ vinctum de domo carceris,
sedentem in tenebris et umbra mortis.

O Key of David,
opening the gates of God's eternal Kingdom:
come and free the prisoners of darkness!

Magnificat

(Latin p. 80; English p. 81)

Repeat antiphon

Prayers of Intercession

May we live this "greater feria" of Advent, in which we recall the great announcement of the Incarnation, as a day of profound silence and careful listening, of awestruck contemplation and concrete determination. May Mary's "yes" to God's plan likewise become our own "yes" of complete adherence to God's plan for us. In this way, he will find hearts that are ready to welcome him on earth today. For this we pray:

> ℟. O Father, source of all joy, make us a dwelling place for your Word.

1. **"Hail, Mary!"** Lord, may this greeting addressed to your entire Church today touch all your sacred ministers as a burst of strength and renewal. Help them accept it with faith and gratitude, that they may receive a new vitality to steadily face the apostolic challenges of joyfully proclaiming the Gospel. For this we pray:

> ℟. O Father, source of all joy, make us a dwelling place for your Word.

2. **"The Lord is with you."** Today, Father, Christ your Son quietly enters into human history as our companion on the journey thanks to Mary's "yes." Give support to the weary legs of so many refugees seeking a hospitable land. Particularly as we draw near to the feast of Christmas, may refugees experience the joy of brotherly and sisterly communion, since we are all part of a single people journeying toward you, our final dwelling place. For this we pray

> ℟. O Father, source of all joy, make us a dwelling place for your Word.

3. **"You will…bear a son."** We thank you, Father, because your immense love continually grants us, who are but parched land, the gift of becoming fertile ground for a joyful and grace-filled maternity. Help us to not fall short of your

expectations. May we be welcoming hearts and a comforting salve for all the poor and the suffering, particularly orphaned and abandoned children. For this we pray:

℟. O Father, source of all joy, make us a dwelling place for your Word.

4. **"How can this be?"** Lord, your surprising call even today in the hearts of so many stirs us to ask, "How?" Help us to follow the example of the Virgin Mary. With her motherly guidance, help us to always accept your holy will with faith and to follow your ways even when we do not understand them, counting only on your grace. For this we pray:

℟. O Father, source of all joy, make us a dwelling place for your Word.

5. **"Behold, I am the handmaid of the Lord."** Father, grant all men and women the joy of transforming their daily lives through the awareness of serving you. May all that we do be an expression of freedom and love marked by a fidelity that never backs down in the face of sacrifice and seeks nothing other than your glory and the good of our brothers and sisters. For this we pray:

℟. O Father, source of all joy, make us a dwelling place for your Word.

Concluding Prayer

Father, out of your immense love you
sent your beloved Son to earth
in search of our wayward selves,
to bring us back to you.
Let your Word of Life
find in us
a free and welcoming dwelling place
like the most chaste womb of Mary,
swift and loving consent,
and complete willingness to cooperate
with your universal plan of salvation.
Through Jesus Christ, our Lord.
Amen.

DAY 6
THE JOYFUL JOURNEY

December 21st

Liturgy of the Word
Song 2:8-14 or Zep 3:14-18a; Ps 32; Lk 1:39-45

Greeting

Celebrant: In the name of the Father, and of the Son, and of the Holy Spirit.
Assembly: Amen.

Celebrant: The grace and peace of Christ, Son of God and Son of Mary, be with all of you.
Assembly: And with your spirit.

Canticle of the Prophecies

(Latin pp. 76-77; English pp. 78-79)

Benedict XVI tells us:

"She herself [Mary], the Mother of Christ and of the Church, . . . teaches us to be a 'manifestation' of the Lord, opening our hearts to the power of grace and faithfully abiding by the words of her Son, light of the world and the ultimate end of history" (Homily, January 6, 2006).

The visitation

✠ A reading from the holy Gospel according to Luke 1:39-45

Mary set out in those days
    and traveled to the hill country in haste
    to a town of Judah,
    where she entered the house of Zechariah
    and greeted Elizabeth.
When Elizabeth heard Mary's greeting,
    the infant leaped in her womb,
    and Elizabeth, filled with the Holy Spirit,
    cried out in a loud voice and said,
    "Most blessed are you among women,
    and blessed is the fruit of your womb.
And how does this happen to me,
    that the mother of my Lord should come to me?
For at the moment the sound of your greeting reached my ears,
    the infant in my womb leaped for joy.
Blessed are you who believed
    that what was spoken to you by the Lord
    would be fulfilled."

The Gospel of the Lord.

Let us meditate together with Benedict XVI:

Mary set out in those days.

"'God is good, he loves us, he knows us, he is with us, with us even to the point that he took on flesh!' This is the *great* joy that Christianity proclaims. . . . Perhaps we Catholics who have always known it are no longer surprised and no longer feel this *liberating joy* keenly. However, if we look at today's world where God is absent, we cannot but note that it is also dominated by fears and uncertainties: is it good to be a person or not? Is it good to be alive or not? Is it truly a good to exist? Or might everything be negative? And they really live in a dark world, they need anesthetics to be able to live. Thus, the words: 'Rejoice, because God is with you, he is with us,' are words that truly open a new epoch. Dear friends, with an act of faith we must once again accept and understand in the depths of our hearts this liberating word: 'Rejoice!' We cannot keep solely for ourselves this joy that we have received; joy must always be shared. Joy must be *communicated.* Mary went without delay to communicate her joy to her cousin Elizabeth" (Homily, December 18, 2005 [emphasis added]).

Topics for reflection and prayer:

Guided by the words of the Pope, let us witness to the joy of Christ.

Mary is "our Mother who communicates joy, trust and kindness and also invites us to spread joy. This is the real commitment of Advent: *to bring joy to others.* Joy is the true gift of Christmas, not expensive presents that demand time and money. We can transmit this joy simply: with a smile, with a kind gesture, with some small help, with forgiveness. Let us give this joy and the joy given will be returned to us. Let us seek in particular to communicate the deepest joy, that of knowing God in Christ. Let us pray that this presence of God's liberating joy will shine out in our lives" (Homily, December 18, 2005 [emphasis added]).

"This world of ours is a world of *fear*: the fear of misery and poverty, the fear of illness and suffering, the fear of solitude, the fear of death" (Homily, December 18, 2005 [emphasis added]). Through Mary, we understand that "if God is absent from my life, if Jesus is absent from my life, a guide, an essential friend is missing, even an important joy for life, the strength to grow as a man, to overcome my vices and mature as a human being" (Address at the Catechetical Meeting with Children who had Received First Communion During the Year, October 15, 2005).

"Anyone who has come across something true, beautiful and good in his life—the one true treasure, the precious pearl—hastens to share it everywhere, in the family and at work, in all the contexts of his life" (Homily at the Vigil of Pentecost Celebration of First Vespers and Encounter with Ecclesial Movements and New Communities, June 3, 2006). "To the extent that we nourish ourselves on Christ and are in love with him, we feel within us the incentive to bring others to him: indeed, we cannot keep *the joy of the faith* to ourselves; we must pass it on" (Address, June 5, 2006 [emphasis added]).

"It is necessary to make it clear that pleasure is not everything. May Christianity give us joy, just as love gives joy. But love is always also a *renunciation of self*. The Lord himself has given us the formula of what love is: those who lose themselves find themselves; those who spare or save themselves are lost. It is always an 'Exodus,' hence, painful. True joy is something different from pleasure; joy grows and continues to mature in suffering, in communion with the Cross of Christ. It is here alone that the true joy of faith is born, from which even they are not excluded if they learn to accept their suffering in communion with that of Christ" (Address, July 25, 2005 [emphasis added]).

"Let us remember in particular, as we look at the streets and squares of the cities decorated with dazzling lights, that these lights refer us to another *light*, invisible to the eyes but not to the heart. While we admire them, while we light the candles in churches or the illuminations of the crib and the Christmas tree in our homes, may our souls be open to the true spiritual light brought to all people of good will" (Audience, December 21, 2005). "The true mystery of Christmas is the inner brightness radiating from this Child. May that inner brightness spread to us, and kindle in our hearts the flame of God's goodness; may all of us, by our love, bring light to the world! Let us keep this light-giving flame, lit in faith, from being extinguished by the cold winds of our time! Let us guard it faithfully and give it to others!" (Homily, December 24, 2005).

Magnificat antiphon:

(classical Latin and English forms)

O Oriens,
splendor lucis aeternae et sol iustitiae:
veni, et illumina sedentes in tenebris
et umbra mortis.

O Radiant Dawn,
splendor of eternal light, sun of justice:
come and shine on those who dwell in darkness and in the
shadow of death.

Magnificat

(Latin p. 80; English p. 81)

Repeat antiphon

Prayers of Intercession

Propelled by the love that filled her, Mary immediately set out to the house of her cousin, Elizabeth. Her eagerness shows how, when we welcome Jesus, it is impossible not to feel a desire to bring him to others, introducing him through humble and active charity. In order to bring this gospel passage to life, let us turn to the Father with faith as we ask him:

℟. Holy Father, make us joyful witnesses to the Gospel.

1. After responding with her "yes" to the divine call, Mary freely and joyfully left to visit Elizabeth. Lord, grant courage and energy to all young people in fulfilling the demands of their vocations. May they be shoots bringing new life to the Church and glory to your holy name. We ask you:

℟. Holy Father, make us joyful witnesses to the Gospel.

2. By the strength of your Spirit, accept and sustain our desire to draw closer to all those who suffer. Wherever we cannot be in person, may our prayers transcend the distance, allowing us to draw all human suffering into our hearts and offer it to you, the God of all consolation. We ask you:

℟. Holy Father, make us joyful witnesses to the Gospel.

3. Lord, we pray for all expecting mothers, particularly those who are tempted to reject their motherhood. Help them find wise counsel and support, that they may overcome any fears and recognize the invaluable gift of life, even in the midst of suffering. We ask you:

℟. Holy Father, make us joyful witnesses to the Gospel.

4. When Mary traveled from Nazareth to Ain-Karim carrying the Word made flesh in her womb, it was the first eucharistic procession in history. Lord, nourished by the bread of life, may we too become eucharistic people capable of authentic

acts of charity, reconciliation, and sharing others' suffering, showing ourselves to be loving toward all. We ask you:

℟. Holy Father, make us joyful witnesses to the Gospel.

5. Father, as we daily accompany through prayer all our brothers and sisters that you call from this life, we also commit them to the motherly intercession of Mary. May she sustain them in the final steps of their earthly pilgrimage and lead them into the Kingdom of Light that your Son reopened for us. May they live peacefully in the resplendence of your face and joyfully in the Communion of Saints. We ask you:

℟. Holy Father, make us joyful witnesses to the Gospel.

Concluding Prayer

O Christ, the Incarnate Word,
you began walking the paths of the world
to bring salvation for all
in the womb of the Virgin Mary.
Help the Church, invigorated
by the power of your presence
in the Sacrament of the Eucharist,
to radiate everywhere the joy of the Gospel.
May she be a light of hope for all
in our earthly pilgrimage toward the heavenly Jerusalem.
Grant this, O God,
you who live and reign forever and ever.
Amen.

DAY 7
A GREAT GOD

December 22nd

Liturgy of the Word
1 Sam 1:24-28; 1 Sam 2:1-10; Lk 1:46-55

Greeting

Celebrant: In the name of the Father, and of the Son, and of the Holy Spirit.
Assembly: Amen.

Celebrant: The grace and peace of Christ, Son of God and Son of Mary, be with all of you.
Assembly: And with your spirit.

Canticle of the Prophecies
(Latin pp. 76-77; English pp. 78-79)

Benedict XVI tells us:

"With Mary, we must begin to understand that . . . we must not drift away from God but make God present; we must ensure that he is *great* in our lives. Thus, we too will become *divine*;

all the splendor of the divine dignity will then be ours. Let us apply this to our own lives" (Homily on the Solemnity of the Assumption of the Blessed Virgin Mary, August 15, 2005 [emphasis added]).

The Magnificat *poem*

✠ A reading from the holy Gospel according to Luke 1:46-55

Mary said:

"My soul proclaims the greatness of the Lord;
    my spirit rejoices in God my savior.
    for he has looked upon his lowly servant.
From this day all generations will call me blessed:
    the Almighty has done great things for me,
    and holy is his Name.
    He has mercy on those who fear him
    in every generation.
He has shown the strength of his arm,
    and has scattered the proud in their conceit.
He has cast down the mighty from their thrones
    and has lifted up the lowly.
He has filled the hungry with good things,
    and the rich he has sent away empty.
He has come to the help of his servant Israel
    for he remembered his promise of mercy,
    the promise he made to our fathers,
    to Abraham and his children for ever."

The Gospel of the Lord.

Let us meditate together with Benedict XVI:

My soul proclaims the greatness of the Lord.

"In the Gospel we heard the *Magnificat*, that great poem inspired by the Holy Spirit that came from Mary's lips, indeed, from Mary's heart. This marvelous canticle mirrors the entire soul, the entire personality of Mary. We can say that this hymn of hers is a portrait of Mary, a true icon in which we can see her exactly as she is. I would like to highlight only two points in this great canticle. It begins with the word '*Magnificat*': my soul 'magnifies' the Lord, that is, 'proclaims the greatness' of the Lord. Mary wanted God to be great in the world, great in her life and present among us all. She was not afraid that God might be a 'rival' in our life, that with his greatness he might encroach on our freedom, our vital space. She knew *that if God is great, we too are great*. Our life is not oppressed but raised and expanded: it is precisely then that it becomes great in the splendor of God" (Homily, August 15, 2005 [emphasis added]).

Topics for reflection and prayer:

Guided by the words of the Pope, let us resolve to make God great in our lives.

"Mary wanted God to be great in the world, great in her life . . . It is important that *God be present* . . . in our community life, for only if God is present do we have an orientation, a common direction; otherwise, disputes become impossible to settle, for our common dignity is no longer recognized. Let us make God *great* in public and in private life. This means making room for

God in our lives every day, starting in the morning with prayers, and then dedicating time to God, giving Sundays to God. We do not waste our free time if we offer it to God. If God enters into our time, all time becomes *greater*, roomier, richer" (Homily, August 15, 2005 [emphasis added]).

"It was thought and believed that by setting God aside and being autonomous, following only our own ideas and inclinations, we would truly be free to do whatever we liked without anyone being able to give us orders. But when God disappears, men and women do not become greater; indeed, they lose the divine dignity, their faces lose God's splendor. In the end, they turn out to be merely products of a blind evolution and, as such, can be used and abused. This is precisely what the experience of our epoch has confirmed for us. *Only if God is great is humankind also great*" (Homily, August 15, 2005 [emphasis added]).

"God is not a remote God, too distant or too great to be bothered with our trifles. Since God is great, he can also be concerned with small things. Since he is great, the soul of man, the same man, created through eternal love, is not a small thing but great, and worthy of God's love. God's holiness is not merely an incandescent power before which we are obliged to withdraw, terrified. It is a power of love and therefore a purifying and healing power" (Homily at the Mass of the Lord's Supper, April 13, 2006).

"Mary's poem—the *Magnificat*—is quite original; yet at the same time, it is a 'fabric' woven throughout of 'threads' from the Old Testament, of words of God. Thus, we see that Mary was, so to speak, 'at home' with God's word, she lived on

God's word, she was penetrated by God's word. . . . Thus, Mary speaks with us, speaks to us, invites us to know the Word of God, to love the Word of God, to live with the Word of God, to think with the Word of God. And we can do so in many different ways: by reading Sacred Scripture, by participating especially in the Liturgy, in which Holy Church throughout the year opens the entire book of Sacred Scripture to us. She opens it to our lives and makes it present in our lives" (Homily, August 15, 2005).

"To the extent that . . . [Mary] spoke with God's words, she thought with God's words, her thoughts were God's thoughts, her words, God's words. She was penetrated by divine light and this is why she was so resplendent, so good, so radiant with love and goodness. *Mary lived on the Word of God*, she was imbued with the Word of God. And the fact that she was immersed in the Word of God and was totally familiar with the Word also endowed her later with the *inner enlightenment of wisdom.* Whoever thinks with God thinks well, and whoever speaks to God speaks well. They have valid criteria to judge all the things of the world. They become prudent, wise, and at the same time good; they also become strong and courageous with the strength of God, who resists evil and fosters good in the world" (Homily, August 15, 2005 [emphasis added]).

Magnificat antiphon:

(classical Latin and English forms)

O Rex gentium et desideratus earum,

lapisque angularis qui facis utraque unum:
veni, et salva hominem quem de limo formasti.

O King of all nations and keystone of the Church:
come and save man, whom you formed from the dust!

Magnificat

(Latin p. 80; English p. 81)

Repeat antiphon

Prayers of Intercession

May the great *Magnificat* canticle, interwoven with the golden threads of the Old Covenant, continually echo in our hearts as Christmas draws near. May it help us experience the joyful expectation of Jesus with Mary's own sentiments, beginning anew our journey as followers of Christ together with her, in humility and gratitude. For this we pray:

℟. Send us your loving Spirit to open our hearts.

1. Lord, everything around us speaks of you and leads back to you. The vastness of the universe reveals your omnipotence and every frail creature shows your humility and tenderness. Grant us the light of your loving Spirit so that we may recognize and serve you in all our brothers and sisters, always yearning to behold your face unveiled. For this we pray:

℟. Send us your loving Spirit to open our hearts.

2. Lord, you know our sorrow for the tragedies of violence and poverty afflicting so many people. Together with Mary and all the most vulnerable of the earth, we ask you to turn your eyes of mercy toward our lost and burdened human race so that we may be open to accepting the gift of peace and joy that you have come to bring on earth. For this we pray:

℟. Send us your loving Spirit to open our hearts.

3. Committing our petitions to the tenderness of Mary, your Mother and ours, we pray for the poorest in our opulent society. May your compassion for human suffering work to change their state, raising a greater awareness of the responsibilities we all have in the face of all forms of indifference and injustice. For this we pray:

℟. Send us your loving Spirit to open our hearts.

4. Having become aware of your remarkable plan of universal salvation, Mary prophetically sang of the greatness of your love. Help us become enlightened and transformed by your Word so that we too may live and work with faith, goodness, and gentleness to instill peace and harmony all around us.

℟. Send us your loving Spirit to open our hearts.

5. Lord, our faithful God, make us able to love gratuitously like Mary, so that our whole life may become an unceasing prayer and song of praise to you who guide the course of history toward its fulfillment in your kingdom of endless light and joy. On behalf of all creation, we ask you:

℟. Send us your loving Spirit to open our hearts.

Concluding Prayer

Lord, as we contemplate with awe
the marvelous work of salvation
you continue to carry out
to restore in us the divine image, marred by sin,
we desire to sing our thanks to you,
filled with astonished gratitude
and joy.
Fill us with your love
and keep our spirits always youthful
and ready to give witness to your faithfulness
with our lives.
Through Christ our Lord.
Amen.

DAY 8
IN A RELATIONSHIP
WITH JESUS

December 23rd

Liturgy of the Word
Mal 3:1-4, 23-24; Ps 24; Lk 1:57-66

Greeting

Celebrant: In the name of the Father, and of the Son, and of the Holy Spirit.
Assembly: Amen.

Celebrant: The grace and peace of Christ, Son of God and Son of Mary, be with all of you.
Assembly: And with your spirit.

Canticle of the Prophecies

(Latin pp. 76-77; English pp. 78-79)

Benedict XVI tells us:

Though he faced hardships and conflict, John the Baptist gives witness by his life to the love of truth and makes us aware that all believers are called to undertake the journey of life in search of truth, justice, and love (see August 18, 2005).

The birth of John the Baptist

✠ A reading from the holy Gospel according to Luke 1:57-66

When the time arrived for Elizabeth to have her child
    she gave birth to a son.
Her neighbors and relatives heard
    that the Lord had shown his great mercy toward her,
    and they rejoiced with her.
When they came on the eighth day to circumcise the child,
    they were going to call him Zechariah after his father,
    but his mother said in reply,
    "No. He will be called John."
But they answered her,
    "There is no one among your relatives who
    has this name."
So they made signs, asking his father what he wished
    him to be called.
He asked for a tablet and wrote, "John is his name,"
    and all were amazed.
Immediately his mouth was opened, his tongue freed,
    and he spoke blessing God.
Then fear came upon all their neighbors,
    and all these matters were discussed
    throughout the hill country of Judea.

All who heard these things took them to heart, saying,
> "What, then, will this child be?
For surely the hand of the Lord was with him."

The Gospel of the Lord.

Let us meditate together with Benedict XVI:

When the time arrived for Elizabeth to have her child she gave birth to a son.

"The central figure in the work of educating, and especially in education in the faith, which is the summit of the person's formation and is his or her most appropriate horizon, is specifically the form of witness. This witness becomes a proper reference point to the extent that the person can account for the hope that nourishes his life (cf. I Pt 3:15) and is personally involved in the truth that he proposes. On the other hand, the witness never refers to himself but to something, or rather, to Someone greater than he, whom he has encountered and whose dependable goodness he has sampled. Thus, every educator and witness finds an unequalled model in Jesus Christ, the Father's great witness . . . This is the reason why prayer, which is personal friendship with Christ and contemplation in him of the face of the Father, is indispensably at the root of the formation of the Christian and of the transmission of the faith" (Address at the Ecclesial Diocesan Convention, June 6, 2005).

Topics for reflection and prayer:

Guided by the words of the Pope, let us open ourselves to a profound relationship with Jesus.

In an age when "the influence of a secularism that exalts the mirages of consumerism and makes man the measure of himself is growing" (Address to the Bishops of the Episcopal Conferences of Lithuania, Latvia and Estonia, June 23, 2006), John the Baptist teaches us not to be afraid to lean on Christ, to long for Christ as the foundation of our lives, and to enkindle within us the desire to build our lives on him and for him (see Address, May 27, 2006).

All believers are called, like John, to embark on the journey of life in a *search for truth, justice, and love*. They are called to become men and women of truth, justice, goodness, forgiveness, and mercy. They will no longer put themselves at the center, asking how something can serve them, but will rather ask how they are serving God's presence in the world. They will learn to lose their life and in so doing find it (see Address, August 20, 2005).

The witness of John the Baptist shows us that "it is necessary to enter into real friendship with Jesus in a personal relationship with him and not to know who Jesus is only from others or from books, but to live an ever deeper personal relationship with Jesus, where we can begin to understand what he is asking of us. And then, the awareness of what I am, of my possibilities: on the one hand, courage, and on the other, humility, trust and openness" (Address, April 6, 2006). The secret of holiness lies in this: *friendship with Christ* and faithful obedience to his will (see Address at the Meeting with Seminarians, August 19, 2005).

Families today are feeling the repercussions of this *relativizing* process that recognizes nothing as definitive, leaving only the self and its desires as the ultimate criterion. Under the guise of freedom, it becomes a prison for each person (see Address, June 6, 2005). It is often possible to find families that have been regrettably scarred by the weakness of the marital relationship, the scourge of abortion, the demographic crisis, and the vanishing concern for transmitting authentic values to children. A modern world not rooted in authentic human values is destined to be governed by the tyranny of instability and confusion. For this reason, every ecclesial community should be a reference point for the society in which it lives, drawing from the Word of God the principles that constitute the essential foundations for edifying a family in accordance with the Creator's plan (see Address, June 6, 2005; Homily, June 3, 2006).

The preaching of John the Baptist is at the same time a call of grace and a *sign of contradiction* and justice for the entire People of God (see Audience, March 15, 2006). Even the duty to *respect life* has today become a sign of contradiction with respect to the prevalent mindset. Since it is an "unavailable" good, human beings are not the masters of life; rather, they are its custodians and stewards. Total respect for life is linked to the religious sense, to that inner disposition with which a human person approaches reality, whether as master or custodian. If creatures lose their reference to God as a transcendent foundation, they risk falling at the mercy of human will, which we know can be used recklessly (see Homily at the Parish of St. Anne, February 5, 2006).

Magnificat antiphon:

(classical Latin and English forms)

O Emmanuel, rex et legifer noster,
exspectatio gentium et Salvator earum:
veni ad salvandum nos, Domine Deus noster.

O Emmanuel, our King, and Giver of Law:
come to save us, Lord our God!

Magnificat

(Latin p. 80; English p. 81)

Repeat antiphon

Prayers of Intercession

The house of Zechariah and the entire surrounding region pulsed with joy at the birth of John the Baptist. May that same joy penetrate our hearts today and anticipate for us the joy of Christ's birth, which is now drawing so close. Abounding in our desire for him, yet aware of our shortcomings and contradictions, we ask to be strengthened by grace so we can leap toward him who is coming to dwell among us. We humbly pray:

℟. Lord, come to us with your grace.

1. Mary served in humble silence and charity at Elizabeth's side as birth drew near. Committing the Church to her motherly intercession, Lord, we ask you to sustain her missionary zeal and make the missionary efforts of her ministers fruitful with graces, so that they may give life in faith to a multitude of spiritual children. We humbly pray:

℟. Lord, come to us with your grace.

2. Revealing yourself as "he who gives graces," you called the Precursor of the Messiah by name from the time he was in his mother's womb. We pray to you on behalf of all peoples awaiting justice and yearning for peace: enlighten the minds and hearts of their leaders. May they be aware of their call to the noble and arduous mission of promoting true unity between peoples based on mutual respect and cooperation. We humbly pray:

℟. Lord, come to us with your grace.

3. The birth of John the Baptist excited great awe in everyone. Lord, knowing that you always surprise us with your salvific interventions, we turn our prayers for Europe to you. May she recognize her Christian roots and oppose the dominant culture of death with a culture that respects life-giving values, thereby creating an open and united society capable of offering our young people a hopeful future. We humbly pray:

℟. Lord, come to us with your grace.

4. After his time of purifying trial, Zechariah's lips were opened and he sang of your powerful salvation. Lord, uniting ourselves to all people being crucified in body and spirit, we ask you to give each of us the strength to accept that suffering with faith and to live it with generosity and meekness, making it a source of graces and blessings for all. We humbly pray:

℟. Lord, come to us with your grace.

5. O God, you sent John to prepare the hearts of your chosen people and welcome the promised Savior. Enlighten us with your Word and bring about a profound conversion within us. May the humble recognition of our sins obtain for us your forgiveness and make us credible witnesses to your merciful love in the midst of our brothers and sisters. We humbly pray:

℟. Lord, come to us with your grace.

Concluding Prayer

Faithful God, Father of our Lord Jesus Christ,
as our time of trial continues
in the advent of our earthly life,
continue to surprise us with your graces,
so that we may walk in your ways with perseverance,
guided by faith,
enlightened by hope,
and moved by love.
Through Christ our Lord.
Amen.

DAY 9
THE FULFILLMENT OF THE WORD

December 24th

Liturgy of the Word
Mi 5:1-4a; Ps 79; Heb 10:5-10; Lk 1:39-48

Greeting

Celebrant: In the name of the Father, and of the Son, and of the Holy Spirit.
Assembly: Amen.

Celebrant: The grace and peace of Christ, Son of God and Son of Mary, be with all of you.
Assembly: And with your spirit.

Canticle of the Prophecies

(Latin pp. 76-77; English pp. 78-79)

Benedict XVI tells us:

"Let us live these last days before Christmas intensely, together with Mary, the Virgin of silence and listening. May she who was totally enveloped by the light of the Holy Spirit help us to understand and live to the full the mystery of Christ's Nativity . . . [and] keep alive the inner wonder in fervent expectation of the celebration of the Savior's birth" (Audience, December 21, 2005).

Mary and Elizabeth's conversation

✠ A reading from the holy Gospel according to Luke 1:39-48

Mary set out
>and traveled to the hill country in haste
>to a town of Judah,
>where she entered the house of Zechariah
>and greeted Elizabeth.

When Elizabeth heard Mary's greeting,
>the infant leaped in her womb,
>and Elizabeth, filled with the Holy Spirit,
>cried out in a loud voice and said,
>"Blessed are you among women,
>and blessed is the fruit of your womb.

And how does this happen to me,
>that the mother of my Lord should come to me?
>For at the moment the sound of your greeting
>reached my ears,
>the infant in my womb leaped for joy.

Blessed are you who believed
>that what was spoken to you by the Lord
>would be fulfilled."

Mary said:

> "My soul proclaims the greatness of the Lord;
> my spirit rejoices in God my savior.
> for he has looked upon his lowly servant.
> From this day all generations will call me blessed.

The Gospel of the Lord.

Let us meditate together with Benedict XVI:

Blessed are you who believed that what was spoken to you by the Lord would be fulfilled.

"'*Magnificat anima mea Dominum*,' she says on the occasion of that visit, 'My soul magnifies the Lord' (Lk 1:46). In these words she expresses her whole program of life: not setting herself at the center, but leaving space for God, who is encountered both in prayer and in service of neighbor—only then does goodness enter the world. Mary's greatness consists in the fact that she wants to magnify God, not herself. She is *lowly*: her only desire is to be the handmaid of the Lord (cf. Lk 1:38, 48). She knows that she will only contribute to the salvation of the world if, rather than carrying out her own projects, she places herself completely at the disposal of God's initiatives. Mary is a woman of *hope*: only because *she believes in God's promises* and awaits the salvation of Israel, can the angel visit her and call her to the decisive service of these promises. Mary is a *woman of faith*: 'Blessed are you who believed,' Elizabeth says to her (cf. Lk 1:45) . . . Mary is a woman who loves" (*Encyclical Letter on Christian Love [Deus Caritas Est]*, no. 41 [emphasis added]).

Topics for reflection and prayer:

Guided by the words of the Pope, let us learn to follow in the footsteps of Mary.

Mary is a woman of hope. "Hope is practiced through the virtue of patience, which continues to do good even in the face of apparent failure, and through the virtue of humility, which accepts God's mystery and trusts him even at times of darkness" (*Deus Caritas Est*, no. 39). "For this very reason, we must be apostles who are filled with hope and joyful trust in God's promises. God never abandons his people; indeed, he invites them to conversion so that his Kingdom may become a reality. The Kingdom of God does not only mean that God exists, that he is alive, but also that he is present and active in the world. He is the most intimate and crucial reality in every act of human life, every moment of history" (Address to the Third Group of Bishops from Mexico on their "Ad Limina" Visit, September 23, 2005).

Mary is a woman of *faith*. "The first person to be associated with Christ on the path of obedience, proven faith, and shared suffering was his Mother, Mary.... Mary is the Mother of the One who is 'the glory of [his] people Israel' and a 'light for revelation to the Gentiles,' but also 'a sign that is spoken against' (cf. Lk 2: 32, 34). And in her immaculate soul, she herself was to be pierced by the sword of sorrow, thus showing that her role in the history of salvation did not end in the mystery of the Incarnation but was completed in loving and sorrowful participation in the death ... of her Son" (Homily on the World Day of Consecrated Life, February 2, 2006).

Mary is a woman who loves. "We see it in the delicacy with which she recognizes the need of the spouses at Cana and makes it known to Jesus. We see it in the humility with which she recedes into the background during Jesus' public life, knowing that the Son must establish a new family and that the Mother's hour will come only with the Cross, which will be Jesus' true hour (cf. Jn 2:4; 13:1). When the disciples flee, Mary will remain beneath the Cross (cf. Jn 19:25-27); later, at the hour of Pentecost, it will be they who gather around her as they wait for the Holy Spirit (cf. Acts 1:14)" (*Deus Caritas Est*, no. 41).

"In the Incarnation of the Son of God . . . we recognize the origins of the Church. Everything began from there. Every historical realization of the Church and every one of her institutions must be shaped by that primordial wellspring. They must be shaped by Christ, the incarnate Word of God. It is he that we are constantly celebrating: Emmanuel, God-with-us, through whom the saving will of God the Father has been accomplished" (Homily, March 25, 2006).

Christmas is a feast of peace. "The Child foretold by Isaiah is called 'Prince of Peace.' His kingdom is said to be one 'of endless peace.' The shepherds in the Gospel hear the glad tidings: 'Glory to God in the highest' and 'on earth, peace'" (Homily, December 24, 2005). Together with Mary, let us foster "the conviction that wherever and whenever men and women are enlightened by the splendor of truth, they naturally set out on the path of peace" (Message for the World Day of Peace, January 1, 2006).

Magnificat antiphon:

(classical Latin and English forms)

Cum ortus fuerit sol de caelo,
videbitis Regem regum procedentem a Patre,
tamquam sponsum de thalamo suo.

When the sun rises in the morning sky,
you will see the King of kings coming forth from the Father
like a radiant bridegroom from the bridal chamber.

Magnificat

(Latin p. 80; English p. 81)

Repeat antiphon

Prayers of Intercession

The time is now at hand! After reliving the anticipation of the Messiah sung by the prophets throughout this Advent season, on this solemn vigil we embark with Mary and Joseph on our spiritual journey to the grotto in Bethlehem. Our hearts are ready to receive the angels' announcement and adore the newborn Child together with the shepherds. Together with all people of good will, we ask:

℟. Come, Lord Jesus, fulfill our anxious anticipation!

1. Our earth, chosen by you as the place for your dwelling among us, is forever familiar with the tragedy of hatred and war.

Speaking on behalf of people of all nations who are weary from prolonged suffering, we ask you for the gift of compassionate dialogue and the peace so longed for. For this we pray:

℟. Come, Lord Jesus, fulfill our anxious anticipation!

2. You were rich and were born in conditions of extreme poverty. You became small and defenseless, desiring to have a need for parents to care for you. We pray for all abandoned, mistreated, and exploited children. May they find families open and willing to welcome them and provide them with warm affection and the possibility of a sound education. For this we pray:

℟. Come, Lord Jesus, fulfill our anxious anticipation!

3. Eternal Word of the Father, you took on our frailty to save humanity, gone astray because of sin. May your birth give back hope to the sick, the afflicted, and the countless poor whose names and faces we do not know. May they hear the Word from the grotto in Bethlehem resounding in their hearts, calling them: "Come to me, all you who labor and are burdened, and I will give you rest" (Mt 11:28). For this we pray:

℟. Come, Lord Jesus, fulfill our anxious anticipation!

4. O Christ our Redeemer, you have come to create a bridge between heaven and earth. May your birth stir a healthy uneasiness in those who based their lives on well-being and do

not know how to look beyond the narrow horizon of earthly happiness alone. May each of them discover how you became man so that we might become children of God, called to your kingdom of holiness and love. For this we pray:

℟. Come, Lord Jesus, fulfill our anxious anticipation!

5. Word of the Father, you come in the silence of our hearts to proclaim your Word of salvation. Help us to keep and contemplate it like Mary, allowing it to shine through in every action of our lives. For this we pray:

℟. Come, Lord Jesus, fulfill our anxious anticipation!

Concluding Prayer

Good and merciful Father,
you have sustained us during this Advent journey.
Grant that we may live to the full
the graces of this blessed Christmas season.
Conform us to your humble and obedient Son,
and help us dedicate our lives
to faithful and generous service,
giving glory to you and helping our brothers and sisters.
Through Christ our Lord.
Amen.

APPENDIX

Canticle of the Prophecies (Latin)

(All strophes from 1 to 7 are recited or sung every day from December 16th to December 23rd. Strophe 8 is added on December 24th, the Christmas Vigil.)

℟. Regem venturum Dominum,
   venite, adoremus.

(The antiphon is recited or sung at the end of each stanza)

1. Jucundare, filia Sion,
   et exulta satis, filia Jerusalem.
   Ecce Dominus veniet,
   et erit in die illa lux magna,
   et stillabunt montes dulcedinem,
   et colles fluent lac et mel;
   quia veniet Propheta magnus,
   et ipse renovabit Jerusalem.

2. Ecce veniet Deus
   et homo de domo David sedere in throno,
   et videbitis et gaudebit cor vestrum.

3. Ecce veniet Dominus protector noster,
   Sanctus Israël,
   coronam regni habens in capite suo:
   et dominabitur a mari usque ad mare,
   et a flumine usque ad terminos orbis terrarum.

4. Ecce apparebit Dominus, et non mentietur:
   si mora fecerit, expecta eum,
   quia veniet, et non tardabit.

5. Descendet Dominus sicut plúvia in vellus,
   orietur in diebus eius iustitia
   et abundantia pacis:
   et adorabunt eum omnes reges terrae,
   omnes gentes servient ei.

6. Nascetur nobis parvulus
   et vocabitur Deus fortis;
   ipse sedebit super thronum David patris sui,
   et imperabit;
   cuius potestas super humerum eius.

7. Bethlehem, civitas Dei summi,
   ex te exiet Dominator Israël,
   et egressus eius
   sicut a princípio dierum aeternitatis,
   et magnificebitur in medio universae terrae;
   et pax erit in terra nostra dum venerit.

The following is added on the Christmas Vigil:

8. Crastina die delebitur iniquitas terrae,
   et regnabit super nos Salvator mundi.

℟. Regem venturum Dominum,
   venite, adoremus.

   Prope est iam Dóminus:
   veníte, adorémus.

Canticle of the Prophecies (English)

(All strophes from 1 to 7 are recited or sung every day from December 16th to December 23rd. Strophe 8 is added on December 24th, the Christmas Vigil.)

℟. Our Lord and King is coming,
O come let us adore him.

(The antiphon is recited or sung at the end of each strophe)

1. Rejoice, people of God,
   and exult with joy, city of Zion:
   the Lord will come
   and there will be great light on that day
   and the mountains will drip with sweetness,
   milk and honey will course through the hills
   because the great prophet will come
   and renew Jerusalem.

2. Behold, the Lord God will come,
   a man from the house of David will rise to the throne;
   you will see him and your hearts will rejoice.

3. Behold, the Lord our shield will come,
   the Holy One of Israel,
   with a royal crown on his head;
   his kingdom will stretch from sea to sea
   and from the rivers to the ends of the earth.

4. Behold, the Lord will appear: he will not fall
   short of his promise;
   if he is not here yet, our anticipation will grow,
   for he will surely come and will not delay.

5. The Lord will come down from heaven like dew upon fleece:
   justice will flourish in his days
   and peace will abound;
   the mighty rulers of the world will adore him
   and all the nations of the earth will serve him.

6. A child will be born for us
   and will be called "Mighty God";
   he will sit on the throne of David, his father,
   and he will be our king:
   he will have royal authority about his shoulders.

7. Bethlehem, city of the Most High,
   the ruler of Israel will come forth from you;
   he, the Eternal One, will be born into time
   and will be glorified in the universe:
   when he comes among us,
   he will grant us the gift of peace.

The following is added on the Christmas Vigil:

8. Tomorrow the evil of the earth will be defeated
   and the Savior of the world will reign over us.

℟. Our Lord and King is coming,
   O come let us adore him.

   The Lord is near,
   O come let us adore him.

Canticle of the Blessed Virgin (Latin)
Lk 1:46-55

Magnificat anima mea Dominum:
et exultavit spiritus meus
in Deo salutari meo;

quia respexit humilitatem ancillae suae;
ecce enim ex hoc beatam me dicent
omnes generationes.

Quia fecit mihi magna qui potens est:
et sanctum nomen eius;

et misericordia eius in progenie et progenies
timentibus eum.

Fecit potentiam in brachio suo,
dispersit superbos mente cordis sui,

deposuit potentes de sede,
et exaltavit humiles;

esurientes implevit bonis,
et divites dimisit inanes.

Suscepit Israel puerum suum,
recordatus misericordiae suae,

sicut locutus est ad patres nostros,
Abraham et semini eius in saecula.

Gloria Patri et Filio
et Spiritui Sancto.

Sicut erat in principio et nunc et semper
et in saecula saeculorum. Amen.

Canticle of the Blessed Virgin (English)
Lk 1:46-55

My soul proclaims the greatness of the Lord;
    my spirit rejoices in God my savior.
    for he has looked upon his lowly servant.
From this day all generations will call me blessed:
    the Almighty has done great things for me,
    and holy is his Name.
    He has mercy on those who fear him
    in every generation.
He has shown the strength of his arm,
    and has scattered the proud in their conceit.
He has cast down the mighty from their thrones
    and has lifted up the lowly.
He has filled the hungry with good things,
    and the rich he has sent away empty.
He has come to the help of his servant Israel
    for he remembered his promise of mercy,
    the promise he made to our fathers,
    to Abraham and his children for ever.